Except The Lord BUILD THE HOUSE

One Woman's Journey through the Valley of Sorrows to the Lordship of Christ

By
CAROL A. CARLSEN

Copyright © 2013 by Carol A. Carlsen

Except The Lord Build The House
One Woman's Journey through the Valley of Sorrows to the Lordship of Christ
by Carol A. Carlsen

Printed in the United States of America

ISBN 9781628715279

All rights reserved solely by the author. The author guarantees all contents are original and do not infringe upon the legal rights of any other person or work. No part of this book may be reproduced in any form without the permission of the author. The views expressed in this book are not necessarily those of the publisher.

Unless otherwise indicated, Bible quotations are taken from the The King James version of the Bible.

Amplified Bible. Copyright © 1954, 1964, 1965, 1989 by the Lockman Foundation.

www.xulonpress.com

TABLE OF CONTENTS

My Heart's Desire 11
The Radiance Of Joy 15
The Crucible Of Sorrow 17
Oh God, I Didn't Mean It! 19
God In Default 22
Push The Magic Button – God Is Mine To Command! . . . 24
The Squinting Struggle To Focus 28
The "I" In The Way 30
The Accusing Search 33
Thinking About Another Baby? 35
Satan Was Deluding Me 38
Walking In Love One Day At A time 41
It Was A Freak Thing 45
From Whence Cometh My Strength 52
Children Are A Gift From God 57
Miscarriage 63
I Claim Your Blessing, Your Promise, God 71
God's Promise Confirmed 74
The Child Of Promise 79
Postlogue 85
About The Author 93

DEDICATION

This book is dedicated to my incredible husband of 52 years – Charles Richard Carlsen, Sr.. He walked this traumatic road with me. He loved, supported and grew with me as God transformed our nominal Christian lives into vital, vibrant and ever-growing walks with the Savior who became the
LORD of our LIVES.

ACKNOWLEDGEMENTS

I also wish to express my gratefulness to my incredible daughter, Cheryl Kaysen. Without her technical skills and love, my 'typewritten' manuscript could not have been submitted for publication.

PROLOGUE

Dear Linda,
I just felt I had to drop this note to you as the Lord has put you on my mind so often and has continued to remind me that although I've been praying for you, I've not shared in the fellowship of your sorrow in a tangible way!

I so well understand the heartbreak you have experienced, the depression you are in the midst of, and the time of questioning and doubting you of necessity will go through because I've been down that dark road, too! I sorrow with you in the loss of your little son. Please let me share with you some of what God allowed me to learn as He refined me in the crucible of sorrow, in the hope of offering comfort for the many trying days ahead...

As I sat there recalling and sharing what had transpired over the past three years in my life, I was both amazed and thrilled. Writing this letter and another one to Diana (who had also lost her baby, a three-month-old son) helped me to see a complete picture of what God had accomplished in my life. I can only look back and say, "No chastening seemeth good, but it yields the peaceable fruits of righteousness..." (Hebrews 12:11 kjv) And I can honestly praise God for a completely new kind of Christian life— a vital, daily growing relationship with the Lord, God, Creator of all that exists, my Father!

Chapter One

MY HEART'S DESIRE

I wanted another baby in the worst way! (Have you ever noticed how many couples who seemingly could care less multiply reprehensibly, or others, who are practicing birth control, somehow slip up and upon discovering pregnancy reproach their fertility vociferously?) Why is it the "have nots" are always in the minority, while the "haves" in the majority enjoy not only our envy, but also our disdain, because we think them undeserving? Why is God so seemingly unfair with His distribution of assets?

Oh, I prayed, how I prayed! If only God would answer this one prayer! But six years of waiting is a long time! It's funny, but the more the time slipped by, the more disgruntled I became. It was sort of like the crude "Coke machine" analogy: As long as I got my Coke, I didn't think about the dispensing machine. But oh, when the soda didn't flow, that machine was the recipient of not only vile thoughts but a few kicks and shakes as well. When God answers prayer, we don't think too much about Him as to Who His is, but only in terms of how He benefits us. When the answers don't come we try all kinds of things to "shake Him up." (We even take matters into our own hands, completely oblivious to His Lordship in our lives.)

That's exactly what I did—took matters into my own hands and went to my gynecologist!

Now, don't get me wrong. There is certainly nothing reproachable about going to the doctor. In fact, it's a perfectly intelligent thing to do. It's just that my spiritual motive was wrong. I wanted to get to the bottom of this so I could point out to God where He slipped up! So I could tell Him that I really didn't need Him—I was smart enough to find the difficulties, correct them and get what I wanted (I overlooked one small fact, the Breath of Life- God gives that!)

I went through countless tests; my husband, Chuck, did too, each one more involved and more costly than the previous one, only to find that nothing appeared to be wrong! There was only one test left, in medical terms an "exploratory laparotomy." My common sense seemed to hold me back—"If every test so far has indicated normalcy and nothing has indicated problems, why should I submit to surgery?"

When my disconcertingly punctual (menstrual) period didn't arrive that scheduled week in April, I held my breath. Did I dare to believe that finally...? When four weeks had elapsed and I was finding myself unnervingly nauseous each morning, I decided it was time to confirm what I hardly dared to let myself believe. Yes! "It was true! My prayer was finally answered! (God and I were now on the best possible terms!) I can remember how eagerly I reinstated an oft-neglected habit—the least I could do was to spend some moments each day reading my Bible and praying (I thought I owed that much to God). So, every day, quite religiously, I did just that! It was good discipline for me.

I can also remember, shortly after verification of my pregnancy, how I, thinking of myself as Hannah of old, offered my baby to God. "This is Your baby, God; I offer him to You." (I always thought of my baby as "him.") "He is Yours!"

The thrill of life is a wildly fantastic thing! The excitement of that first feeble flutter within, then the amazement as one's anatomy adapts itself to the advancing activity of a growing miracle just has to make motherhood one of life's most sacred times!

I thrilled as each new stage approached. And, with my nursing background, I marveled over and over at God's handiwork.

Nine months seemed like an eternity. When December arrived, the time seemed to stand perfectly still. Even the busy flurry of Christmas activity was not enough to keep my mind off my impatience. Christmas Eve finally arrived. (We Scandinavians celebrate then.) The house was full of relatives and my six-year-old, Cheryl, wide-eyed with anticipation, pestered, "Please, Mommy, just one, can I open just ONE present?" Chuck complied by allowing her to open the special box of Chinese puzzles we had set aside for just this purpose. She was kept busy for the interim.

Christmas Eve, for us, follows a specified traditional pattern. About 6 P.M. we all sit down to a grandly festive table laden with the customary smorgasbord of hot and cold foods (including at least fourteen different types of cookies baked only at this time of year). Between dinner and dessert the head of the household always reads the Luke 2 account of the Christmas story. This is followed by prayer and the singing of Christmas Carols; each one present selects his favorite. The dessert that follows is perhaps the only dessert of the year the children present would like to skip. You see, after dessert everyone adjourns to the festivities of gift opening. (As a child, I can recall making the same comment as my daughter Cheryl, "I'm too full, let's not have any dessert tonight, okay?"

I remember easing myself gently into a red velvet barrel chair and smiling as I thought of that childhood taunt, "Carol, Carol, fat as a barrel!" I was so pregnant it seemed my skin would burst around my middle. I can recall thinking, "Mary, I don't know how you did it—riding all the way to Bethlehem on that donkey. If it had been me, the poor animal would have collapsed!"

Cheryl joyously distributed the small mountain of gifts to the eleven eager recipients (the children always have this "job"). What fun it is to hear the squeals of pleasure. Everyone is a child at Christmas!

As I put Cheryl to bed that night she remarked, "Mommy, we're getting our best present after Christmas this year—our baby!" How candid and refreshing are those offhand remarks of children. Cheryl was surely thrilled at the prospect of a new baby. Everyone she knew had brothers or sisters; now she was soon to become a big sister too!

We marked off the calendar each day, anticipating the seventh of January—due date! On January 5th at 9:30 A.M. I had what I hoped would be my last appointment with Dr. Henry Saphier (a unique and beautiful person—God bless him) before delivery. Upon examination, Henry frowned and said, "Carol, you're bleeding. It may be your 'show' (an indication of the onset of labor) but maybe not. Go home, go to bed, and call me at 7:00 this evening." I went home hoping labor would commence immediately. Through the day there was more and more bleeding, but not enough to alarm me. I forgot all about calling the doctor, so at 7:15 the phone rang. "You were supposed to call me, Carol," scolded a mockingly gruff voice. "How's that bleeding?" "A bit heavier but no contractions yet." "Well, hop in the car and meet me down at the hospital; I'd like to check you out again," he said, matter-of-factly. "Okay. When?" "As soon as possible." I called Mother and she arrived ten minutes later, visibly upset. "Oh, Carol, what's wrong?" "Everything's going to be fine. Don't worry! Maybe you'll be a grandma again tonight!" Mother waved goodbye with tears streaming down her face. "Oh, Carol!" she cried. Chuck and I drove off to Englewood Hospital.

Chapter Two
THE RADIANCE OF JOY

All I could think of as we drove the short three miles to the hospital was, "I hope he'll induce me—I can't wait for this to be over!" I tingled with excitement. "A baby, oh, a baby to cradle in my arms! I'll know soon if it's a boy or a girl." I met Dr. Saphier on the Labor and Delivery floor. As he examined me, I couldn't wait to hear him say, "I'll induce you and we should have a baby by morning." I was not at all prepared for what he did say. "Carol...It looks like an abruptio" (the beginning of a separation of the placenta from the uterus; the completed separation is called placenta previa). I searched my memory of nursing school days and recalled that immediate surgery would be required.

I then saw blood-soaked sheets and realized the extent of my hemorrhaging. A second obstetrician confirmed Henry's diagnosis. "We are going to operate immediately!" "Caesarean section," I thought dejectedly.

I asked the nurse what the fetal heartbeat was. Her answer told me of the immediate jeopardy of my baby. I was quickly "prepped" and "draped." "We have to do this with a spinal, Carol, said Dr. Saphier, as he knew I had shortly before eaten my dinner (the danger of aspiration is too great with general anesthesia when food has recently been ingested).

As the doctor tested to see if all was numb, I can remember feeling a slight sensation as he scratched my abdomen. He started to cut and I screamed, "I can feel it, I can feel it!" The tension of the moment was fantastic, so the assisting obstetrician yelled, "Put her out, Henry—you don't need that!" Oh, how I grasped for the minimal amounts of anesthesia coming from that mask. "Relief from pain!!!" I felt my head hyper-extend in an attempt to inhale more of its euphoric contents!

I heard the cry—my baby!

"What is it?" I asked.

"A boy, Carol. A beautiful boy." You can imagine the joy of wanting a son and having God grant that desire!

He was so beautiful, so perfect, a little Chuck even down to the white fuzz of Chuck's curly hair! I thought I would burst from the joy, the amazement, the pride, the love!

As they wheeled little Craig away to the nursery, I couldn't wait another second. "Thank you, God! Oh, thank you!" The nurse smiled knowingly at my outburst.

Chuck, Mother, and Susie Cramer (my darling next-door-neighbor and 30-year nursery nurse at Englewood Hospital who had been as excitedly anticipating my delivery as she had her own grandchildren) saw me in the hall prior to the stretcher-ride to my room on the maternity floor above.

"Isn't it wonderful? A boy!"

I had already forgotten the pain! My baby was here!

I don't know how I got to sleep that night; the radiance of my joy lit up the room like daylight!

Chapter Three

THE CRUCIBLE OF SORROW

The night passed slowly and uncomfortably.

"That miserable I.V.! Why in the world did they have to put it in the bend of my arm!" I complained angrily. I put on my light to signal the nurse.

"Yes?" asked the efficient voice.

"This I.V. is infiltrating. Can't you change it to another location? My arm is numb from being stretched out on this board, too!" "Let's see," she soothed as she monkeyed with it. "I think it will be okay now. I'll be back later to check it." Whisk! She was gone! I was still aching—-

Stop complaining! I scolded to myself. A few more hours and you'll be feeding that precious little boy! I guess I talked myself into forgetting the discomfort by thinking of how I was going to enjoy our little Craig, of how wonderful it would be to be a family of four. Suddenly it was morning! I had actually slept a few hours! I was quite surprised to see Dr. Saphier so early.

"Hi, Carol, how are you doing?" he questioned softly.

"I'll be fine if you'll get rid of this plumbing in my arm! That was a dumb place to put it, you know!"

"Aw, come on Carol, we were in a hurry and that's a real good vein! I'll speed this up and it should be done in fifteen minutes, okay?!" (He didn't tell me he had ordered another one when this ran out!)

"I'll count those minutes and if it's longer, can I turn it off?" I quipped naughtily.

"Wise guy!" He retorted, "I'll see you later!" Shortly after Dr. Saphier left, my breakfast arrived; milk, tea, and Jell-O. How do they expect me to eat this, I wondered. I'm lying down, I can't shift my weight, my arm's suspended, I ache all over, I hate milk, tea makes me sick in the morning, and Jell-O, cherry Jell-O, yuck! (What a frame of mind!)

Suddenly a cheery lady in a salmon-pink volunteer coat appeared! "Good morning! May I help you?" I thought it very strange to see a volunteer so early in the morning, but I dismissed the odd feeling by saying, "I guess I do need help." Somehow she got every bit of that liquid into me.

A lovely nurse's aide helped me clean up and brush my teeth.

"Why all this attention?" I mused. My roommate, who had delivered shortly before me, must have sensed it, too, because she stated rather flatly, "Are you some kind of VIP with all this attention?" I dismissed the pinch of apprehension by laughing lightly; "Guess that's the difference between surgical and normal deliveries."

Next a nurse came in and pulled the curtain halfway around my bed. "That's better; the sun can blind you in this room!" ('What sun? I wondered'). "That's queer," I mused, and just as I was beginning to succumb to the apprehensions of the peculiar goings-on a familiar figure walked through the door. My pediatrician, John Bell, walked in. My jubilant "Hi!" to him brought a sudden rush of perspiration and a beet-red flush to his face — my heart stopped as I listened to his seemingly interminable explanation, as he groped for the only words I actually heard, "...and I'm sorry, but your son expired at eight this morning." I collapsed in his arms!!

Chapter Four
OH GOD, I DIDN'T MEAN IT

"No! No," I sobbed, not believing what I was hearing. "Do you know what came into my mind that very moment, the very first thought, the very first utterance?" It was "Oh, God, I didn't mean it! I didn't mean it!" The prayer of consecration I had prayed as Hannah did, for God to have Craig, came rushing into my head! It was a figurative prayer—but God had taken it quite literally.

They had me transferred off the maternity floor to GYN lest the crying of babies cause even more trauma. I lay completely alone, seemingly forgotten. No nurse came to check on me, not even a maid to clean! Panic struck! I couldn't reach the signal to call a nurse, I couldn't move! Every part of me throbbed—the incision, my numbed arm with still another I.V. running into it, my head, for I was reacting to the spinal anesthesia with an intense spinal headache. And my heart, my spirit, was broken!

"God! God! Where are You?" I screamed. I cried hysterically. No one heard, no one cared!

When I finally came to myself, I thought of Mother, Oh, she wouldn't forget me, ever! "How can I reach that phone?" It was on the same side of the bed as my boarded-up arm, and the bed was still elevated to high-stretcher height (for easy transferal from stretcher to bed). Therefore, the phone was on a stand lower than the bed. Also, the guardrails were still up. With one reckless lunge after another, I finally managed to pull myself sideways. The phone was just out of reach, so I pulled open the drawer on the stand so I could get leverage on the table. I pulled with unknown strength and the stand moved. Now that precious communicator was within reach. How I dialed Mother's number with my left hand and all that pain I'll never know, but even more inexplicable was the fact that the telephone was already hooked up. Usually a patient must contact the operator so charges can be properly assessed before patient usage. (I'm sure God provided for this!)

"Mother, I need you..." I sobbed so hard I choked on the words. I don't remember what she said; only that somehow because I'd reached her she would be able to help. As I lay waiting and agonizing, I saw that my "Foley" catheter was backing up and my I.V. was infiltrating again. I couldn't do anything about the "Foley," but if I only could reach the drip control on the I.V.! I struggled, but my strength-was gone.

"Let me die!" I thought for an abandoned moment of utter despair.

Just then Chuck walked in! My darling Chuck! The realization shattered me—I had not once considered his reaction, his sorrow, his perplexity—I was too busy wallowing in my own. "I'm sorry, I'm so sorry," I wept, half-ashamed of my rejection of his need and half guilty because somehow the death of his son must be my fault.

He fumbled for some words but none came; he just embraced me helplessly and soaked me with his tears. This communication needed no verbalization. It was that strange mingling of love and sorrow.

Dr. Saphier arrived, and I blurted out my woes, showed him my "Foley" and my ballooning arm.

"G—D—- it!" he swore angrily. "I'm sorry, Carol." He pulled out the I.V. and strode quickly up the hall. I heard his angry voice barking reprimands and orders. I'd never seen him angry, as gentleness is his characteristic. "What the h—- is wrong with this floor? Why hasn't anyone checked on her?" His voice trailed off and soon my room was swarming with personnel. From then on I was given priority service.

With the morphine taking effect, I gradually started to calm down and my pain subsided.

Chuck and I talked of many things. Then he left to make funeral arrangements. I was alone again.

"God, I didn't mean it!" started to ring in my ears again. I began to think of how many other prayers I prayed that I really didn't mean, either!

"Who are You, God?"

"Why did You do this to me?!"

I sobbed myself to sleep.

Chapter Five

GOD IN DEFAULT

In the days that followed, my mind was constantly bombarded with incomplete thoughts—angry, resentful thoughts. I tried so hard to put them out of my mind; I even denied that they were actually there at all. Oh, the frustration of guilt feelings!

I was angry—angry at God—when I came right down to it. (But how can a Christian entertain such thoughts? So I suppressed these feelings until they exploded and burst out!)

"You know how much I wanted that baby, God!"

"Why did you allow a pregnancy if you were going to take him right away? Why me? What have I done to deserve this? After all, look what I do to serve You—You owe me something for what I've done!" I then proceeded to list in my mind all of the avenues of service I was involved in.

"God, You're supposed to be Love—well, I resent Your lack of it. In fact, in all honesty, I'm not even sure You really do exist!" There! I said it—I let the honesty of my thoughts and feelings all out! I could go on and on, but some of those thoughts are better left unsaid! (Tsk, tsk, Christian?)

I was brought up in a fundamentalist Christian home. I know "Jesus Loves Me" was the first song I ever learned, and table grace was surely memorized before nursery rhymes!

My parents taught me about Jesus from infancy and I made a commitment to Christ at a youth rally by going forward to confess my sins and to accept Him as my Savior at age 12.

Almost all my recollections of living a Christian life as a youngster are that because I was now a Christian, I could NOT do anything everyone else could do! I couldn't go to the movies, dance, play cards, read movie magazines, play on Sundays, smoke, drink—the list was interminable! What's wrong with movies? brought a very uninformative "Christians don't do that!" "Why?" "Jesus wouldn't want to find you in the devil's house if He came, would He? You must do only what He wants you to do, if you want to go to Heaven! In my mind the things emphasized were the negatives I shouldn't do to avoid wrath and Hell, and the positives I should do to earn God's pleasure and heaven. All my life was spent balancing that scale—I envisioned God just waiting for it to tilt the wrong way and handing me over to Satan. I practiced being a Christian (and a pretty good one, at that!). I was a Sunday School teacher, I was a Pioneer Girl's Guide, I was an officer lithe Women's Missionary Fellowship, I was church soloist, I was, I was, I was! That's exactly where my problem was: I was, I did, I didn't, I came to God when I needed. I MEASURED UP TO WHAT I THOUGHT I SHOULD BE AS A CHRISTIAN AND WHAT OTHERS THOUGHT I SHOULD BE, TOO!

Now, here I find myself with all these un-Christian, unloving, ungodly thoughts! Please get this picture—good Christian Carol, sitting in the midst of her good Christian life, weighing her good Christian deeds—FINDS GOD IN DEFAULT! "God, if You really love me, if You really are in control, PROVE IT!" I shook my fist in His face! I had dared to challenge God!

Chapter Six

PUSH THE MAGIC BUTTON – GOD IS MINE TO COMMAND!

This was probably the most meaningful prayer (if an agonized challenge can be considered a prayer) I'd prayed since I knelt in contrition as a newborn babe in Christ. I thought back over my attitude toward prayer.

Praying was a Christian duty. I did it perfunctorily because a Christian is supposed to, even when he doesn't want to, or feel like it.

It was a way of stamping God's okay on what I did, or was about to do ("God, I'm going to start a Bible study—bless it!"). I never consulted Him first, to see if that's what He wanted me to do.

He was my private "genie"—I poured out my needs and wants, and "Errand Boy, God" was supposed to grant each one!

Most of my prayers went something like this:

"Dear God, I need this, help me do this, I want that, forgive me for this...Bless me, my family, my friends. Oh, yes, thank You for being my Savior. In Jesus' name, amen."

The long or the short of it always consisted of succinctly listed requests, lots of requests, lots of blessings, and a few thank-you's thrown in—topped off with the passwords that got the prayer to God's ears, "in Jesus' name."

Suddenly I was beginning to see something quite startling! The God I knew was just what my "Hannah" prayer had been, FIGURATIVE! He was not LITERALLY my God at all! I didn't live for the purpose of glorifying Him! "Lo, I am with you always..." I didn't take that literally; that was figurative—God, of course, was somewhere out there, seeing all I do, but I didn't have the actual, literal knowledge that <u>HE IS LORD</u>! I had been living my Christian life so that I could earn "brownie points" to please God so that in my warped, twisted conception, I could get what I thought God should give me because I deserved it! I was seeing myself, analyzing my Christian life, and coming up with— "Jesus is my Savior, so I'm on the winning team." That meant winning the game, collecting the prize and getting the glory! Because I'm a winner, I have influence—I just push the magic button, pray the magic prayer, and God is mine to command! Wow! Was that a shocking eye-opener! Good Christian Carol was neither good, nor very Christian!

PRAYER

When I converse with God in Prayer
Of what does it consist?
Petition for my needs and wants
Succinctly in a list?
When I kneel down before His throne
What cause has brought me there
Is it the place of " last resort" -
My call to Him in prayer?
Have I exhausted each resource
Before I finally say,
"Dear Lord, please help with this request
-there is no other way!"

(I seem to think He's far away
Unless I call Him thus;
I seem to think He doesn't care
Untill I fret and fuss!)
He's numbered every hair of mine-
He sees the sparrow fall-
Is He then unaware unless I
In frustration call?
Oh foolish child, when will you learn
the Father loves you so?
There's not a portion of your life
He doesn't fully know!
Then why not come before His throne
with words He wants to hear—
With praises and thanksgivings,
Sweet music to His ear!
Come to glorify the Lamb
Whose blood was shed for you,
Come in exultation of the
Lord of Life anew!
Come in worship-adoration,
Ceaseless joyful praise,
He who made all things exist is
Keeper of my days!
He understands, He knows my needs
Before I think to ask,
And tending my necessities,
His choice parental task!
My wants are something else, indeed-
He'll answer in His way,
His grace is so available-
Sufficient for each day.
So, rather than petition,
I'll offer Him my love-
Rather then lament my wants,

Sing praise to Him above!
To worship, laud, acclaim, extol-
The purpose of my prayer,
The rest of life- Oh, help me Lord
Entrust it to Thy care!
© Carol A. Carlsen 3/11/74

Chapter Seven
THE SQUINTING STRUGGLE TO FOCUS

One doesn't challenge the Living God without dramatic results!

My attention was constantly being drawn to a deep analysis of my "Christian" life. A restlessness, a real search of my attitudes, motives and behavior riddled me—but at the same time something else was happening to me. Not a miraculous, then-and-there revelation, but a subtle, gentle, warm feeling that I was slowly being surrounded by love. My bitterness and resentment somehow seemed to be melting away and I was finding myself quite defenseless without these weapons—being enfolded in the center of the experiential Presence of "LOVE."

You can't fight against Love! Carol was about to get the answers she wanted!

As the manifest presence of Love was encompassing me, I began to take a long look at this God I called Father, and this Jesus I called Savior. For the first time I saw the awesomeness and majesty of the Creator of all that exists. I considered the lilies of the field, the sparrow, the numbered hairs on each head, the stars of the sky, the sands of the seaside. Together with David of old I asked searchingly, "Who am I, that You, God, should be mindful of me?—Who am I, that You, God, You, should come to me and make Yourself known?" All the things that I had known so matter-of-factly about God since childhood (known in my mind, that is) came rushing into my being, my soul, my spirit— I now KNEW God; I was experiencing HIM!

Jesus, my Savior, the world's Savior—God's only begotten Son (I thought how God, the Father, must have felt the agony of death, too). He sent His only Son to die. Somehow the Easter story had new significance as I could feel in a sense the sorrow of God in my own sorrow for my son!

The Love—LOVE—LOVE! The unspeakable reality of God's love electrified me!

In the time that followed, as I poured myself out in confession, that cloud of Love that surrounded me on the outside started to flood over me on the inside, too—the Holy Spirit manifested Himself! The Savior had now become LORD! It was like squinting when you walk from the dark into the light and momentarily struggle to focus. Then it comes—everything bright and perfectly clear! I saw Who God is and I saw myself in the reality of my humanity, the created being, the so-loved, redeemed, created being, the clay in the Potter's hand! Praise and thanksgiving overwhelmed me and I was rejoicing in the midst of sorrow! Peace, a peace unlike anything I'd yet experienced completely inundated my entire being! I was not the same Carol—God was not <u>mine</u>—rather, I was <u>His</u>! It was not what I could do <u>for</u> Him—it was what He could do <u>through</u> me! I knew as reality that GOD'S LOVE SURROUNDS ME LIKE A CLOUD AND NOTHING GETS TO ME UNLESS IT GOES THROUGH HIM FIRST! That was the beginning of an entirely new Christian life for me!

Chapter Eight

THE "I" IN THE WAY

*P*erhaps some explanation is needed at this point lest it sound as though I am completely deriding my religious background. I am not. Both Mother and Dad were truly "born-again" Christians, as were my grandparents. They were all very active in the Bible-believing churches they attended. My mother's father was a fundamentalist preacher, an Evangelical Free Church minister, and my Dad was a lay preacher and singer. Our home and family life was Christ-centered. We had a family altar with daily devotions. My sister and I were surrounded by Christian doctrine. All worldliness was labeled such and eschewed. We were cloistered from the world. Our social life was centered in the church, with church people, and the world was kept as far from us as possible (except in terms of evangelization). Our church preached salvation at every service, Sunday morning, evening, and Wednesday prayer meeting. The most important thing was to be "saved" and to tell everyone else how they could be "saved," too! Here is where my confusion appears to have its roots. Somehow my conception seemed to be that the ultimate goal was salvation; but after a commitment to Christ I had to work at protecting that salvation lest I lose it again. I never remember hearing a sermon on Christian growth — everything geared to the Christian was in terms of what was or wasn't acceptable conduct for the maintenance of the "Christian" life. The most important thing was to win souls. Yet the "witnessing" I recall seemed to be all in negatives. One must attack as a soldier and "capture" souls. This was done primarily by pointing out where this one or that one differed in crucial theology. This accomplished, the Christian was then in a position to enlighten! The result, of course, was the psychological reaction of self-protection. How dare the "Christian" attack the "non-Christian" and expect the non-Christian to turn to Christ?! The backlashing given to the Christian was viewed as expected suffering for the sake of Christ, inflicted by Satan, and was to be counted as gain!

Also, Christians, it appeared, seemed to be on constant review to other Christians. Criticism of such things as too-long hair, too-short skirts, reaction to trauma, ability to pray or testify, etc., seemed to be the content of private discussions and the Christian was judged of his fellows by a particular standard. Those measuring up the highest were considered the best Christians.

I never remember hearing a sermon preached on the Person and work of the Holy Spirit. The God I knew was "BI-UNE," Father and Son. The Holy Spirit was mentioned only in the final benediction "in the name of the Father, the Son, and the Holy Spirit..."

Therefore, whether it was intended or not, I was engulfed in a theology that truly centered on Christ and His salvation, but which made me work to maintain it and displayed very little love because it kept me too busy "doing to earn, not doing out of love." As I saw it, although Christ accomplished salvation and said "It is finished," in my concept it wasn't — I had to work to Sustain it. Somehow, that made me of some tangible worth to God — I was accomplishing something good and thus pleasing fellow-scrutinizers as well as God.

Therefore, I was deserving of everything in Christ and I could reverently use God to my advantage.

I'd memorized "our righteousness is as filthy rags," (Isaiah 64:6 kjv) but somehow that didn't cover my efforts for God (the things I did in my own strength to suit my own purpose, which I offered to God to sustain my Christian status). Now the Holy Spirit showed me that the only thing that maintained my salvation was God's love, the same love that arranged the plan of salvation and carried out the redemptive work of Christ on Calvary's cross. Salvation, which I always had understood to be the "end-product," the "ultimate goal," I came to see as only the beginning— the door to a fantastic, vital, moment-by-moment relationship with God, the Father, MY Father ("Daddy" if you please, and that is not irreverent; it denotes the personal, loving expression that encompasses all a father is to his child).

I started to understand that God didn't want what I could do—He wanted ME— He wanted to make me the expression of Himself! That's where His Holy Spirit, that Person of the Trinity I knew so little about, came in. I came to understand that my salvation experience, which made me a new creature in Christ through the workings of the Holy Spirit, also equipped me to live a new life (not just a good life by my own efforts). I guess the best way to explain it is as one would describe the electrical system in a new house—all the circuitry is ready, but there is no power until the main switch is turned on! All my Christian life had been lived lighting ineffective candles here and there when all the while I had a never-ending source of power all ready for operation, but I never pulled the switch, nobody ever told me how, I didn't even know I could!

Chapter Nine

THE ACCUSING SEARCH

"Linda, there's another troublesome area I'd like to share with you...looking for the one place to point your finger and say, 'Here is the reason why this happened!'

"I'm sure you have found yourself searching accusingly for the things you might have done differently."

"If only I had..."

"Why didn't I..."

"Wow! Satan really gets in there and hammers away! 'When a guy is down, try to crush him completely!'"

I was plagued by thoughts like that. These thoughts were added to by well-meaning friends who, acting as Job's comforters, would bring up certain actions (okayed by my doctor) and insinuate that because I'd done these things I'd endangered my baby.

In retrospect, I really don't think I would have done anything differently!

I know I was more prudent during my pregnancy with Craig than I had been during my pregnancy with my first-born, Cheryl. Cheryl survived under conditions at least as critical as Craig's. You see, in my seventh month of pregnancy with Cheryl, I developed several kidney conditions, beginning with pyelonephritis (an infection in the kidney), progressing to kidney stones, and ending with uremia (which is often fatal, as toxins which should be excreted are returned, instead to the blood and carried through the body).

I remembered the excruciating pain of the kidney stones and determined to be very careful during Craig's progression to avoid the recurrence of them. It was determined that the position and pressure Cheryl exerted before birth caused blockage in the ureters, which led to kidney stones, which in turn led to uremia.

Thus, I made sure I got off my feet and rested several times a day. Chuck elevated the foot of the bed slightly to reduce a pressure build-up while I slept. Besides, after waiting six years to become pregnant again, I tried to do all I could to insure a healthy pregnancy!

Life and death are ultimately not ours to control! If we delude ourselves with such thinking as "I should have" or "I shouldn't have," we create unnecessary hardships for ourselves, which interfere negatively with other family relationships.

Indulging in this type of thinking is not only futile as it can never restore life, but it can instead make existing life miserable, even unbearable! It's the perfect snare Satan delights in entangling us in! Because what has been can never be again; time cannot be reversed, but it can be relived in regretful memory ending in despair.

Chapter Ten
THINKING ABOUT ANOTHER BABY?

"Linda, I'm sure you're probably thinking about wanting another baby—and most likely with mixed emotions,
"I need another baby to fill this void!"
"But what if I lose this baby, too?"
"How can I live through nine months of fear like that?"

I know that every time I saw a pregnant woman or an infant, my heart ached! I wanted a baby—any baby—to take Craig's place! Then, as tears welled up, I'd think I couldn't stand to lose another one (or my own life, for that matter, as I was now classified a "high risk" pregnancy candidate). My desire to try again was further complicated by difficulties in conceiving (we had waited four years for Cheryl and another six for Craig). A rather hopeless situation to be found in, I thought.

Adoption—that's an answer! Chuck and I had looked into this quite seriously before my second pregnancy. However, where we were living in the East, the waiting list was at least four years because of the "pill" and abortion reforms. After Craig's death, when I decided to look into it again (note the "I decided;" I never consulted the Lord—My, how much I had yet to learn!) my inquiry was replied to with an "I'm sorry, we don't even know if we can fill the applications we have, and we are not accepting any more..." Shortly after this discouraging news, I was given some information about a young girl who planned to put her illegitimate baby up for adoption at birth. I inquired and was put in touch with a lawyer who would make "arrangements" for us. Chuck and I were rather amazed at the mercenary attitude of this lawyer, whose sole function was making these kinds of "arrangements" coast to coast. Among other things, one of his analogies comes to mind:

"If you went out and totaled your car in a collision, you wouldn't think twice of spending four or five grand to replace it—isn't a human being worth at least as much as a good car?"

We didn't have $5,000 to "buy" a baby, and we didn't like the sound of what we seemed to be getting, into.

Chuck and I went to see another lawyer concerning what we had been offered, and were told that these "adoption" actions bordered on the illegal. If we became involved, we would be taking a chance. The second lawyer said his own ethics would not permit him to involve himself!

Of course, that ended that; but I was still in the same situation as before; in fact, worse. I was disillusioned and depressed.

Finally, when my desire for another baby exceeded my worst fears, I decided I'd be willing to try again (as though I was the one in control).

Convincing Chuck was another matter. He was as frightened, if not more so, than I was. Craig's death had crushed him.

"Honey, we have Cheryl. She's healthy and happy. I'd rather have one healthy child and a healthy wife than risk another child and lose you in the process! What good would it be for Cheryl to grow up without a mother?"

We bantered the pros and cons back and forth, and finally I said, "Look, Chuck, our conceptual problems are so great we should pray about it, and if God grants life...we'll leave it up to Him!"

So we earnestly put the matter before the Lord. Amazingly, in spite of my previous difficulties, I became pregnant almost immediately!

Chapter Eleven
SATAN WAS DELUDING ME

Shortly before verification of this pregnancy, I received the autopsy report I'd requested. It revealed that Craig had died from a respiratory condition known as Hyaline Membrane Disease. The cause of this syndrome is not known, nor is there a known antidote. There are procedures, which may be helpful, but thus far research has revealed little except that if the baby can hold its own for 72 hours, it recovers with seemingly no after-effects. The knowledge of the cause of death brought some consolation in that there had been speculation as to a congenital heart anomaly and other conditions. Now at least I knew that genetic factors were not involved. Craig had been a perfectly normal baby in every other respect.

My third pregnancy was a physically exhausting one in that I found nausea and vomiting a daily occurrence for almost the entire gestation. However, it's the emotional factor I'd like to share with you. Those fears came fast and furious from the first pangs of nausea until the day I was scheduled for a repeat "C-section'. At first I denied them, saying that I was delighted to be pregnant again. Little by little, however, I began to indulge those fears and gradually I was becoming a literal nervous wreck.

One day, as I was driving my car to pick up my Aunt Clara, who had been doing some work at our church, I found myself preoccupied with vivid thoughts of a grossly disfigured baby, then of my own excruciating death. The more I thought, the more real it became until suddenly I became aware of the physical distortion of my vision. I slowed the car down and tried to focus. As I approached the parking lot of our church, my vision started to dim, blackening from the peripheries toward the center. I felt like I was driving into a funnel. Then...total darkness! Panic-stricken, I jammed my brake foot to the floor. The car jerked my body harshly and I became aware of a violent headache beginning. "What is happening to me?" I thought, terrified. As Aunt Clara approached my car, parked awry in the middle of the lot, she asked, "Carol, what's wrong? You're snow white!"

She took the wheel, and as she drove home I related what had happened. While I was speaking an exact reversal of my symptoms occurred. By the time we arrived home my full vision had returned and all that remained of the phenomena was that violent headache. I don't remember anything else about the occurrence except that I gratefully collapsed in the arms of sleep for many hours.

Several weeks later the same fears plagued me, even more detailed, more grossly horrible. This time I was at home.

"I'm going blind!" I screamed. Indeed, I <u>was</u> blind! Chuck drove me to the hospital. New fears piggybacked the old. "What if I never see Chuck again, or Cheryl, or this new baby? How can I keep my house or cook?" In that instant I realized just how precious the sense of sight really is! Why must something be taken away before we truly appreciate its value? Chuck led me to the Emergency Room and then to the examining room. While awaiting Dr. Saphier, I became aware of the onset of another headache. As its severity increased nausea overcame me and violent, projectile-like vomiting occurred. After the vomiting my vision slowly cleared.

Following Henry Saphier's examination, a neurologist was called in for consultation. Nothing!—They found nothing physically wrong! "Hysterical blindness." My fears culminated in an emotional hysteria!

It was then that I realized something—I was refusing to give God this part of my life! Satan was deluding me into thinking that my emotions were mine to control. Either God was the Giver of Life and in full control or I was playing God and maintaining life by sheer will power—obviously I was a poor impersonator!

Satan truly is a master at deception, and he plays to win—fear and worry are two of his most successful weapons in undermining the Christian. For to fear is to negate trust in God and it has awful torment. To fear is to doubt and to call God a liar, literally—for by it we say <u>God is not life, God is not omnipotent, God is not love, God is not capable</u>.

"Okay, God, You're in charge—all the way! Nothing will happen to me that You don't allow! Help me to rest in that." Well, that wasn't the end of fear. I mean, fears kept right on coming. Satan is in there hammering away. What I do mean is now I knew what to do with fear. It boiled down to two choices— succumb to its temptation and make myself hysterical or give it over to God by acknowledging His sovereignty. As many times as I gave it over to Him, that many times He took the fear away and replaced it with His peace.

God is Love, and He was teaching me to walk in His love one day at a time. "Perfect love casteth out fear." (I John 4:18 kjv) Little did I know of the supreme test He was preparing me for. Not knowing what lies ahead is surely one of God's practical blessings...

Chapter Twelve

WALKING IN LOVE ONE DAY AT A TIME

*K*nowing truths about God with your intellect are one thing — applying the truths of God in practical day-by-day living is something else. More about this later.

I found myself being constantly reminded of the attributes of God and the promises He made to us. I delighted in the Book of Psalms and often found myself praising just as David — almost feeling as one with David—rejoicing in God's presence, loving Him!

I was starting to see myself with new eyes. My experience with fear made me take closer looks at other areas of my life that I was "controlling."

How thankful I am that God doesn't reveal our problem areas all at once—it would be too devastating. The Holy Sprit (at least in my case) seemed to work in one area at a time. Almost invariably He showed Himself to be the answer to a particular need before I saw that I had that need myself. It appeared that as soon as my mind accepted His Lordship in a certain area a practical test came to see if I could literally apply my learning in daily experience.

Take for instance the "holier than thou" attitude I had toward Chuck (of course I wouldn't admit that it existed, but the evidence screamed above my denial). How insidiously it had crept up on me. I had learned that the reason Father had made me His child had little to do with me, other than my coming to Him, but everything to do with Him—it was His LOVE. My goodness, my works, had not made me worthy; rather, I was an object of mercy, undeserved mercy. Yet, here I was assessing my good works and puffing myself up. I compared myself to Chuck and, of course, I rated so high on the scale that I couldn't even see Chuck. (The areas I picked for comparison were obviously the ones I excelled in.)

I complained: "You're supposed to be the spiritual head of this household so why don't you..." and I rattled on with my list. I was subtly knocking him, down and belittling him by inferring how much I was doing for God. I expounded on my successes and wondered why Chuck wasn't even enthusiastic.

At that point I proceeded to "write" the script for how we should operate our Christian home. I assigned the roles and began playing my part. Chuck, however, didn't play his. The more I insisted the more defiant he became.

When it was obvious that Chuck wasn't measuring up, I took the martyr's part and started to fill in his gaps so we could have a smoothly operating "Christian life" together. I was so caught up in this pious little fiasco that I began thinking that Chuck was "backsliding" because he refused to be what I thought he should be! In fact, he was becoming so negative that he would even answer "no" before I finished asking a question.

"What's wrong with you, Chuck? You're so hostile I can't even talk to you any more! You'd better get yourself straightened out with God!" I said haughtily one day. He glared and shot back vehemently, "You get yourself straightened out!" What a thing to say to me! Here I was doing everything I could! I was even doing his job! How could he say such a thing to me? It's amazing how Satan can blind the unwary Christian, but it's a million times more amazing how God can take what Satan intends for evil and turn it into something good! Here's what happened.

Through most of our married life I had entertained this "holier than thou" attitude because of my "good works" syndrome. But it had always been a rather quiet under-current. Now it was rearing its head with all its ugliness.

"Lord, You have to help Chuck. He needs to have a deeper life in your Spirit; convict him and help him to be the man You want him to be." I prayed with all the sincerity a wife could have for the man she loved. You can imagine the great shock I had when I read I Peter 3:1-4 (amplified):

In like manner you married women be submissive to your husbands—subordinate yourselves as being secondary to and dependent on them and adapt yourselves to them. So that even if any do not obey the Word (of God) they may be won over not by discussion but by the (godly) lives of their wives, when they see the pure and modest way in which you conduct yourselves, together with your reverence (for your husband, that is you are to feel for him all that reverence includes) to respect, defer to, revere him; (revere means) to honor, esteem (appreciate, prize) and (in the human sense) adore him; (and adore means) to admire, praise, be devoted to, deeply love and enjoy (your husband). Let not yours be the (merely) external adorning with (elaborate) interweaving and knotting of the hair, the wearing of jewelry or changes of clothes; but let it be the inward adorning and beauty of the hidden person of the heart with the incorruptible and unfading charm of a gentle and peaceful spirit, which (is not anxious or wrought up but) is very precious in the sight of God.

I was totally devastated! Chuck wasn't the spiritual head of our home because I had usurped his place! His reaction was perfectly natural—he resented my confrontation, he reacted to my superiority" and he rebelled totally at all I was doing that threatened his rightful position!

It's utterly awesome to see the creepy things that scurry to hide when light is turned on in a previously dark place. They were there all the time but what the darkness concealed, the light revealed.

I had learned with my mind that my works didn't count for my righteousness, but I was not applying that "knowledge" in life. I was still putting the works foremost and to top it off I was trying to push Chuck into that same mold! Our marriage was ripping at the seams because of the pressure I was exerting to accomplish my "pseudo-spiritual thing."

It wasn't easy to put into practice what God had shown me. My pride and my ego were threatened every step of the way. But I wanted to be the kind of wife that God desired me to be. I had the wish, the will to try—now God through the Holy Spirit, could operate and accomplish in me what my human nature could not, "for it is God that worketh in you both to will and do of His good pleasure."

What happened? Just what I had wanted all along. Chuck took his place as spiritual head of our home. Instead of his previous antagonism and negativism, he began to grow. He began to develop characteristics I had never dreamed he had. I couldn't believe what was happening. I got out of his way and God's way and our marriage took on a new dimension.

Chapter Thirteen
IT WAS A FREAK THING

The holidays approached. Thanksgiving led into Christmas, and as I prepared for the festivities I thought back to the previous year. "An exact duplication," I thought. It was almost as if last year had not even happened for here I was, just as pregnant, wearing the identical maternity clothes, baking the identical Christmas cookies, preparing the same foods, decorating the same tree, wrapping the same types of toys and gifts, singing the same carols... Maybe last year never happened; maybe it was all a bad dream. So real was the blockage that I found myself thinking, "Yes, in three weeks I'll have my little Craig!" I visualized a beautiful, blue-eyed, fuzzy, blond-haired baby boy bundled up in a blue blanket and cradled in my arms. "My baby, my baby!" I sobbed. "He would have been almost a year old, he would have been so excited, this would have been his first Christmas!" My thoughts went wild, succumbing totally to a mother's sorrow! Oh God!

As I began to calm down, I became aware of some rather well-placed kicks! "Ouch!" I responded to the hammering against my ribs. My emotional state was being violently protested by the other occupant of my body! "Thank You, Lord, for Your obvious reminder. You are in control of life–my life, this new baby's life, and of course, Craig's life. You've taught me so much this past year—I'm not at all like the Carol of last Christmas!" I found myself just praising the Lord and repeating strangely familiar words: "This is Your baby, God—I give it to You." As Hannah of old, I offered for the second time another baby to Him! Only this time I was fully cognizant of what such an offering could mean. Yet, with a new understanding, a new confidence, I could truly say, "Thy will be done!"

It was a jubilant celebration—Christmas—and the joy of Jesus just goes on and on! New Year's is rather a peculiar time. Almost all of us reflect on the year past by totaling up the scores on accomplishments and failures. We check out the tally and confidently resolve to do better in the coming brand new year. A new year is another chance, and there's something so reassuring about another chance. There's a kind of confidence because we see the previous one as the practice run. Now we know the strengths, the weaknesses—we can make it on another chance! Oh, how sure we are of ourselves on New Year's!

I can remember myself briefly looking back, seeing where I'd been and marveling at God's patience with me. Now that was behind; ahead was the year that would make up for the past. Eagerly I anticipated it! The remembrance of our beloved Craig's birthday was marked by a lovely bouquet of blue and white carnations with baby's breath. Not one word did Chuck speak to me, nor I to him; our eyes and hearts spoke to each other in a way that words cannot express. January 5th had come and gone!

I was scheduled for a repeat Caesarean section on January 16th. How anxious I was for all this waiting to be over! As I prepared to go to the hospital the evening before delivery, my excitement was slightly tinged with apprehension. "What if I never awakened again?" (I don't like the idea of being "out.") I thought about the recuperation needed after surgery, the discomfort. It was all quite fresh—it had happened exactly a year and ten days ago. "What if...?"

"You have a lovely baby girl, Mrs. Carlsen!" the recovery room nurse told me as I started to revive from the anesthesia.

"That's nice," I mumbled, quite aware of that 'slipping in and out of it' feeling which accompanies the twilight before the complete consciousness returns. The next thing I remember was being rolled off the stretcher onto the bed in my hospital room.

"Ready...one, two, three, over we go!"

The nurse hooked up all my plumbing and I was left alone. I looked around. "A private room?" I was a bit disappointed. It's nicer to have a roommate to share with. My thoughts went from one thing to another as drowsiness often dulled my brain.

"A baby girl—Christa Lynn—I'm surprised, Lord; I thought surely You'd have given another- son, to replace Craig, I mean."

Isn't it funny how our minds work—we seem to do lots of planning and assuming on our own. I suppose I was slightly disappointed for the moment. But, "Lord, thank You for Christi; we'll love her just as much as we would have Craig!" Pink bouquets started to arrive. The beauty and fragrance of God's handiwork cheered an otherwise nondescript room.

"Congratulations, Carol!" A loving voice called out. My pastor, Stanley Dokken strode to my bed and clasped my hand. "We're so happy for you!" His smile vibrant, sharing, thrilling, rejoicing with us. He had been a true source of comfort and encouragement in our dark days—a man gifted of God with such compassion and love such as I've never seen manifested in any other. He knew personally our heartache as he himself had buried two infant sons. As he read from God's Word and shared and prayed, the Spirit of God flooded that room with joy and peace.

My baby was in such good hands. My dear next-door neighbor, Susie Cramer, had awaited the moment of Christi's arrival almost as eagerly as I. She cared for her from her birth as much like a new grandma as like the neonatal specialist she was. Everything was perfect!

Or so I thought. I rested in my contentment, unable to see the furrowed brow of my dear neighbor as she detected labored breathing in my Christi or the anxious eyes that watched her baby-pink complexion turning cyanotic (blue).

Dr. Bell knocked quietly on my half closed door, his worried expression communicating before his words "Carol," he spoke as gently as he could, "we're having some problems with little Christi..."

"Respiratory?" I broke in. "Yes. It doesn't look good, Carol..."

"We can just as well be optimistic as pessimistic, can't we?" "Surely, but I'd like to have her examined by the pediatric Chief of Staff." "Fine. Go ahead." And he left the room.

Alone again, I momentarily felt like waves were crashing down on all sides and I couldn't fight them, so I saw myself drowning. But then I seemed to hear a gentle, "My child."

"My children, Mine, MINE!"

"Yes, Lord, I am Yours, Yes, Lord, Christi is Yours, too. I trust You in life or death." My thoughts and intimate conversation with my Lord were interrupted a while later by another subdued voice.

"Hi, Carol. I just came back from the nursery. Looks like trouble again." Dr. Saphier looked down at the floor as he spoke.

"Can I see her, please?"

"Sure, I'll get you a stretcher right away."

As the nurses pushed me down the hall toward the nursery, my mother was coming up the hall. I saw the tears in her eyes as she reversed her direction and followed me back.

It Was A Freak Thing

My sister, Darlene, met me at the nursery window and she clutched my hand.

"Carol..." she broke down and couldn't say any more. Susie was there. She smiled a weak smile and went about moving the isolette so I could get a better view of little Christi. She tilted her wee body and I could see her chest fill and dip with struggling breaths.

"Oh, God. She's so little, so helpless, so otherwise perfect. Please—please—let her live?" my heart cried out.

We stayed as long as we could, and reluctantly I let them roll the stretcher back to the room. It was a long afternoon. Chuck and I tried to encourage each other, as we were surely not ready to believe God, would take two children in a row! As he kissed me goodnight, Chuck said, "Don't worry. Everything will work out."

An hour or so later I heard my door slowly open; two of the most dejected men stood looking at the floor. Henry looked up and I saw his face. It was livid and his lips were purple. He spoke softly, "Carol, we did our best."

John Bell, red-eyed and choked with emotion, tried to explain what had happened. "It's a freak thing. I don't know that it's ever happened before—two full-term, otherwise healthy babies succumbing to Hyaline Membrane Disease."

I later discovered why Henry looked as he did. It seems that when Christi was going sour and in real trouble they had called both my pediatrician and my obstetrician, but Henry lived much closer to the hospital and arrived first. He had driven unthinkingly "down" a busy one-way "up" street in his hurry, and when he arrived at the nursery he had given mouth-to-mouth resuscitation to my Christi for 45 minutes. Nurses there said it was as if he refused to let her die.

The tears overflowed and ran down my cheeks. I could think of nothing except, "Father, teach me to understand." There was no anger, no bitterness, just submission. "Life and death ultimately are not in your hands, Doctors. I know you did your best." "Carol, shall we call Chuck?"

"No, let me do it."

"Are you sure you can?"

"Yes. I'd rather tell him." Then my heart sobbed, "Oh, Chuck, how will you be able to bear this—a son first, and now a daughter!" My mind started racing through how I thought he would react. Then suddenly I was overcome with, "He's Chuck's God, too! He'll see us both through this!"

My thinking stopped abruptly as Henry said, "What's your number; I'll dial it for you."

Chuck answered. "How are you, honey?" he asked. "I don't know," I answered, half weeping. "What's wrong?" I could hear the panic building in him. "She's gone, Honey. He has taken Christi home." There was silence and then soft sobs as both of us, separated but united, shared the sorrow that only He who is acquainted with our griefs could assuage.

Finally Chuck said, "I'm coming down now. I want to be with you." A while later Chuck walked in. It was nearly midnight, both chronologically and emotionally. As he embraced me not one word was spoken. And I remembered the last time, one year ago. It was as if time had stood still!!

One's mind does funny things at times like this. As if to negate unwanted circumstances, I asked, "Is it raining out?" I had noticed that Chuck's jacket was quite soaked. "No," he answered. "But I met Dr. Saphier downstairs and I guess it's a combination of our tears. He feels so terrible!"

My thoughts went to Henry and John. How hard this was for them, too. They were both fathers as well as doctors, and I know that their skills as professionals were heightened by their feelings as fathers in trying to save Christi. Somehow, having the same thing happen twice in a row to them, as well as to us, must have hurt deeply.

I've often wondered what must go on in the inner beings of doctors who, having done all they could, must stand by and see it all come to naught. Life and death must surely stir up thoughts to deep to acknowledge. But God says, "Be still and know that I am God." (Psalm 46:10 kjv) It is He that has made us, and not we ourselves. We are His people, and He wants us to know Him personally, as a child, his father. His love is so great that He sent and sacrificed His own Son, the Savior of each of us who will believe and accept. Surely He, above all, knows the path of sorrow—He walked it with a cross.

Chapter Fourteen

FROM WHENCE COMETH MY STRENGTH

The piano tuner was just finishing up when the conversation began. Soon he was saying, "Some God! How can you say there's a God if He destroys little babies, lets the world be ravaged with disease, lets people kill each other. No! There's no God, at least not the kind you believe in. That's not love!" I tried to share with him how God made us with attributes of will and choice, and how the trauma and evil on earth are the result of sin. But he wouldn't listen. His eyes glowered with anger, and I couldn't help but wonder what sorrow had passed through his life to make him so terribly bitter. His parting words were, "And I feel sorry for you because you're so deluded..."

"Oh Father, how do I handle something like this?" I was numb with solicitude for this one whom the Father loved so much.

"How many others react as this one?"

Then I thought back to myself—of my reaction to Craig's death. I was so angry. I was so bitter. But God...

Those words, "BUT GOD..." I had to trust that God had some purpose in that conversation. I may never find out here, but someday I expect to see where it all fit in, for the "BUT GOD" in that man's life. The means that the Father uses to bring us to Himself and the means He chooses to make of us what He wants us to be, are as unique as the individual himself.

Who can understand the depths of God's love? He who loved us, as unlovable, unloving, unreceptive as we are, does so until we come to the point of saying, "What must I do to be saved?" It is then that He makes us a "new creation" in Christ because we simply come, confessing our sins and accepting the saving grace of Jesus! He puts His Holy Spirit within us and equips us to live unto Him. And we can truly say, "For me to live is Christ." (Philippians 1:21 kjv) Before Christ we just existed— creations alienated by sin—now we live as children destined to live with Him eternally, when He comes to take us home to Heaven.

The months that followed Christi's death were the time when I buried myself in studying, seeking to learn as much as I could about applying the Word of God practically in day-by-day living.

We can know and memorize God's Word, but it doesn't amount to much if it isn't applied in living situations, and if it doesn't start to change us so Christ and the fruits of His Spirit are seen in us.

How much I realized I needed to be taught how to feed myself. Oh, sure, I could understand the "hamburger" part, but I longed to get to the day of a "sumptuous feast!"

That doesn't happen overnight. We Americans are very spoiled; everything is based on immediacy. Much of our food is instant; our machines take away three-fourths of our effort in tasks. We go quickly and we get quickly. But there is no such thing as an instant Christian maturity. We are given all the tools, but God says "Study to show thyself approved unto God, a workman that needeth not to be ashamed, correctly interpreting the word of truth" (II Timothy 2:15 kjv). We have to provide willing effort. But how does one start?

I have a very big gripe to share here. I believe that many in the Christian church today have made a grave error. They are so preoccupied with "salvation" that they think of Church success in terms of quantity—how many they have brought to Christ for redemption, the number baptized and recruited as members, etc. But how many churches have follow-through programs to help new Christians grow and get established in the faith and strong enough to feed themselves? (The Church I am a member of, is a wonderful exception! Our Pastor has put in place a one-on-one program for growth of new converts.) I believe that an evaluation of "quantity" would often reveal very poor quality!

Oh, how many "obstetricians" we have in the Kingdom of God, but how few "pediatricians" there are to see to it that new babes are weaned off the milk and on to the meat of God's Word. That's why we find so high an incidence of "infant" near-mortality and retardation among new converts. I speak from experience, because for sixteen years my spiritual retardation was gross! Teaching takes effort and time and personal involvement. That's too big a price to pay for the preacher who already is scheduled up to next year.

We have to be aware of the fact that too many Christians have relinquished their charge to "Ye are My witnesses," and instead, sit complacently back to passively enjoy as spectators the sport of "How many souls has Pastor won?" Do we actually feel that because we pay him, he should do our job for us? Therefore, many Pastors concentrate their efforts totally on evangelism leaving little time for feeding and shepherding new believers so they, in turn, can be strong enough to be effective witnesses to the lives they touch in the world.

Imagine! If pastors were able to assign mature elders and deacons to patiently nurture and instruct and share with new believers until they understood who they are in Christ and how to practically "work out their own salvation" (Philippians 2:12 kjv) day by day in the nitty-gritty of personal relationships, tension, anxiety, grief, etc., what changes we would see! If only they would!

The apostles and the early church saw this need and dealt with it decisively: "In those days when the number of disciples was increasing, the Grecian Jews among them complained against those of the Aramaic-speaking community because their widows were being over-looked in the daily distribution of food. So the Twelve gathered all the disciples together and said: It would not be right for us to neglect the ministry of the word of God in order to wait on tables. Brothers, choose seven men from among you who are known to be full of the Spirit and wisdom. We will turn this responsibility over to them and will give our attention to prayer and the ministry of the word. This proposal pleased the whole group. They chose Stephen, a man full of faith and of the Holy Spirit; also Philip, Prochorus, Nicanor, Timon, Parmenas, and Nicolas from Antioch, a convert to Judaism. They presented these men to the apostles, who prayed and laid their hands on them. So the word of God spread. The number of disciples in Jerusalem increased rapidly..." and a large number of priests became obedient to the faith.

It is apparent the ministry of the Word of God was paramount in their thinking. Dare we be less concerned today? No newborn baby ever survived without food, nor has one survived that was told "feed yourself." No, indeed, we carefully care for, love, and provide for every need. We progressively offer stronger and larger bits of food until the baby is capable of using utensils himself. Even then we supervise until we are sure that spoon-gets the food to the right place! That could start a whole different–ballgame because that one person would be an effective soul winner, who would bring "new babes" to the church to be taught how to grow and produce;

pretty soon there would be an active body of living stones fitly joined, instead of a passive pile of unmortared pieces.

The church is not a building we come to; it is a living structure we are part of. We don't come together to act like Christians as part of an exclusive club. We come together to gain the strength and teaching to be the kinds of Christians who will make an impact on the everyday world we're living in! If we're not doing that, something's wrong!

Chapter Fifteen

CHILDREN ARE A GIFT FROM GOD

What happens when you lose two children? The first thing you get is advice; the first person to advise you is your doctor. My Henry said, "Cool it, Carol. You've had two Caesarean sections within a year. Your body needs a rest. In addition to the physical shock, there's the emotional one to consider, too."

"Are you suggesting that I go on the pill?" I asked. "No-no!" he laughed. "You're the last person in the world I'd put on the pill! With your luck you'd probably develop an embolism the first week! But there are other means. I'm serious, Carol; give yourself at least a year before you even consider another pregnancy."

"Do you think I want to try again?"

Henry smiled. "Well, Carol, anyone who's been through the hell you've been through and comes out on top like you have..."

"It's only the Lord's strength that brought me through it," I said softly.

"I know, I know. You're some kind of a gal! I should have more patients like you!"

I could see the value of his advice, and so I followed it. Next, your family offers advice. Mother was the second one to get in line.

"Please, Carol, don't ever get pregnant again! You've been through enough! Who's to say that you might not be the one to die in childbirth next time?!"

Other family members made similar comments. My friends shared this attitude, too. Soon I was thinking, "Of course, they are right. My Cheryl needs a mother more than she needs a brother or sister." I deliberately put all thoughts of another child out of my mind, as was only common sense for a woman in my situation.

I was relaxing one afternoon, browsing through a "Woman's Day" magazine, and my eyes fell on an advertisement which pictured a lovely, wholesome-looking young woman tenderly caressing a beautiful baby. The tears rolled down my face as I was overcome with emotion.

Is it wrong to want another baby? God gave me these maternal feelings and my instinct is only natural. Lord, I'm listening to prudent human advice, but am I listening to You?"

I had a problem, and as I had come to learn, the only solution was in putting it before the Lord and waiting for His answer! Waiting for an answer is an exasperating experience. We want our "yes's" immediately! We'll even accept "no's" because they put the subject to rest; but "wait's" are just not what we are willing to hear!

I had no choice, however. My own "better" judgment led me to take advised precautions and assume "no" was the answer until I was sure what the Lord wanted.

I can remember often praying and arguing my case, hoping to show God the pros and cons of both positions—imagine, me trying to enlighten the Giver of Life—had I learned nothing? Was there no carry-over? As I read and meditated on His Word, I tried to manipulate Scripture to apply to myself, but I never had the peace of knowing I was in God's will. My prodding just didn't hurry my Lord. It took a few months to see the futility of my childishness. "Wait on the Lord, be of good courage, and He shall strengthen thine heart; wait, I say, on the Lord" (Psalm 27:14 kjv). So I waited, impatiently. My mind was distracted in the beginning of May as I thought of our anniversary coming up in June—I had nothing to give Chuck. Our medical expenses left us with little extra in the financial department. This particular day, as I sat and reminisced of the many things that had transpired in our eleven years of marriage. I thought back to the beginning. What if I had known what lay ahead for us? Words began to take form in my mind and I was compelled to take paper and pen. When I put the pen down, this is what was on the paper:

Dearest Chuck,
Darling—when I married you—
Eleven years ago
I never once considered that
my love for you could grow.
I loved you with a new-pure love
That overflowed my heart;
I thought I knew the ultimate
From then 'til death us part.
I could not know what lay ahead—
On that our wedding day
Nor would I care—for I had you
To plan and share the way.
I dreamed with new-bride ardor
Of the perfect life we'd lead;
Ours would be a journey
Free from trouble, want or need.
How soon I would discover
Those dreams could not come true—
For I was far from perfect—
And Darling, so were you.
We had our petty arguments—

Our raging tempests, too.
We learned that life together
Meant resolving points of view.
We gained new insight of ourselves
That first year long ago;
We needed cultivation if our love
Was ere to grow.
Those stubborn stones of selfishness—
Defiant weeds of will,
Those cutting thorns of unkind words
Would seek our love to still.
That first year was the practice ground—
The time for us to learn
That in ourselves we could not think
That untilled soil to turn.
God would have to show us how—
For He, Himself is love.
And as we yielded unto Him—-
He filled us from above.
Our love indeed began to grow—
For God, Himself, was there;
Slowly, surely, pruning us—
The object of His care.
Looking back across those years
Of varied situations—
Those times of sunshine and of rain
And trying tribulations.
We see the way that God allowed
These things—plus growing room—
Produce in us a flower fair,
A fragrant, tender bloom.
Could I love you even more
Than on our wedding day?
HOW MUCH MORE you'll never know
For words can't fully say!

*Nor can I measure what I feel
For you within my breast;
I only know when God gave you —
He gave to me His BEST!*

*With all my love,
Carol
© Carol Carlsen 6/23/73*

My sister, Darlene, brought it to her office and had it typed in script-type. Then she found a long, thin, walnut frame for it— the one in which it still stands today.

Other things now distracted my attention, for Chuck had made a very difficult decision—to leave his position after eight years as an elementary school Physical Education teacher. Several of the schools in which he taught had impossible, facility-less conditions to work under, and the stress of maintaining a feasible program, coupled with the tragedies we'd undergone, left him with a pre-ulcerative stomach condition. In the midst of seeking to comfort Chuck, I

waited on the Lord to give me words to encourage him. It was at this time the Father chose to speak Psalm 127 — the words fairly jumped off the page: K.J.V.

*Except the Lord build the house,
They labor in vain that build it.
Except the Lord keep the city- the watchman waketh
but in vain. It is vain for you to rise up early
and to sit up late to eat the bread of sorrows.
For so He giveth his beloved sleep.
Lo, children are a heritage of the Lord
And the fruit of the womb is His reward.
As arrows are in the hand of a mighty man
so are the children of thy youth.
Happy is the man that hath his quiver full of them...*

I couldn't believe what I was reading—."children are God's gift—a quiver full?" (Cheryl may have been a handful, but she was certainly not a "quiver full.") The Lord spoke emphatically and indelibly to my mind and heart. I was shaking and weeping as I was hearing, "Carol, my blessing, my gift to you—take my gift— believe what I have said—I will build the house, your house..." Then came the peace, the utter tranquility that comes with knowing God's will and being in the midst of it. He had spoken and I had heard!

Chapter Sixteen
MISCARRIAGE...

When I shared with Chuck what had happened, I had expected him to be as excited as I was. He wasn't, in fact, he was quite negative.

"Honey, I don't want to try again. I've been through this twice, and that's two times too many!" he said firmly.

"But if I'm willing to go through it again—and I wouldn't unless I really believed God—won't you at least pray about it?"

"Let's not talk about it any more." Chuck turned and left the room.

I was stunned. It hadn't occurred to me that Chuck would be anything less than enthusiastic. After all, the Lord had told me and I believed Him—why couldn't Chuck? The more I thought about it, the more upset I became. What was wrong with Chuck, anyway? Where was his faith? Besides, I was the one who had the most to lose. After all, I was the one to suffer the physical discomfort of pregnancy, the greater discomfort of surgery and recuperation, in addition to the emotional strain; whereas his part would only be emotional. If I was willing, why couldn't he be also!

"Lord, shake Chuck up and show him how foolish he is!" I stormed. I didn't dare talk to Chuck for fear of his exploding, so I sat silently and seethed! As I sat, I became aware of the radio, the music was barely audible, coming from the kitchen. I got up and walked toward the kitchen thinking to make myself a snack. As I approached, the words of the song hit me full blast: "Oh, the peace that Jesus gives—Never dies, it always lives..." Peace? Some peace! "Lord, why do I always get in the way? Why do I always think I can do it myself? Thanks for the reminder—I needed it! I can only have peace by trusting You and I know You'll work it out!"

Several days passed and I never brought up the subject or even hinted at it; I just prayed and waited.

One evening, as Chuck and I were relaxing and watching TV, he got up and quietly turned the set off. "Honey, how much does having another baby mean to you?" he asked suddenly. I was completely taken aback.

"A lot," I blurted out, not even thinking. "Why?"

"Well, I've been thinking about it a lot. Do you realize what you're asking me to do? Can you understand what it means to me? Do you know the agony I've been through? I love you— I've seen all the suffering you've been through. Do you know what it does to me to watch you suffer and not be able to help you, just to stand helplessly by and feel guilty because in a way I'm the cause of it? I can't let it happen again." Chuck buried his head in my chest and sobbed. He released all the feelings that had been bottled up inside him. It was difficult for him to share those deep thoughts. I think somehow men don't want to seem so vulnerable; they want to be the strong refuge for their wives and families. But it was necessary for me to know, because for the first time I could understand some things about my beloved Chuck that had heretofore been unknown. I was sick when I remembered my many angry thoughts about Chuck's attitude (I was so glad I hadn't hurt him by verbalizing them). Oh, how much I had to learn! I was such a fool! I was so immersed in my own feelings that I so often overlooked Chuck's. Selfishness pops up in so many areas and ignorance is no excuse. Our love deepened that night—there was new understanding and insight. As we knelt together before our Lord in prayer His Spirit flowed through us. As Chuck closed his prayer he prayed, "And Lord, if You mean to bless us with another child, I'll trust You, even as Carol does!" We fell asleep in each other's arms, more in love than ever before!

I didn't even know I was already pregnant, but I knew something was wrong from the amount of sudden bleeding! Dr. Saphier looked at the contents of the small jar I brought him and confirmed, "A miscarriage." He scheduled the D&C for the following Saturday morning. It happened so quickly I couldn't think—or didn't want to. When I came home from the hospital (I'd seen so much of that hospital I was sick of it) I sat down on the sofa and cried. My mind and heart were churning. What happened? Did I dream what You said? Am I turning into some kind of religious fanatic who conjures up religious experiences? Where are You, God? Where are You?'"

Chapter Seventeen
MORE COMPLICATIONS

A wall had been erected between the Lord and me. For several weeks I simply sulked. My attitude was, "This is all Your fault, Lord, and if that's how You're going to treat me, I don't need You!"

My Bible started to collect dust, for every time I walked by it I said, "I'm not talking to You, Lord, and I don't want You to talk to me, either!"

During the day my thoughts would go to God, but I stopped myself by saying, "Lord, go bother someone else, I'm not talking to you—remember?"

Funny how I always addressed Him as "Lord"—my heart knew, but my mind was angry!

When I think of it now, I can correlate it to some of my little girl's reactions to her mommy's correction. I can see her angrily clasp her arms across her chest, narrow her eyes, plop down as hard as possible on the nearest chair, defiantly swing her head away from me and announce haughtily, didn't hear one word you said!"

I couldn't get angry, for the sight of this little mite acting in such a way was just so ludicrous I simply had to turn my back so she wouldn't see me laugh!

Somehow, I seem to think that God must have had exactly that reaction to me—for I was just as ludicrous!

Chuck stopped me short one day. "What in the world is wrong with you, Carol? You're impossible!"

Of course I was impossible. I was fighting to hold on to my false ego. I was hurt and confused. Although I didn't enjoy being this way, my pride prevented me from doing what I knew I should—talk to the Father about it.

I broke down and haltingly told Chuck how I felt, how hurt I was because I assumed everyone would think I just imagined what God had said and talk behind my back, saying, "Boy, Carol is some glutton for punishment!" "Did you imagine it, Carol?" Chuck asked gently.

"No, of course not. Do you think I'd risk going through all this again if I wasn't positive?"

I was so forceful in what I said that I surprised myself.

"Well, do you think God changed His mind?" he asked, with a slight hint of teasing.

"No, silly. God doesn't change His mind once He's said something!" I answered dogmatically.

"Well?"

"Well, what?" I asked coldly.

"Well, why are you so upset then? If God hasn't changed, who has?"

The hint of teasing in Chuck's voice irritated me. I turned to explode at him. Then I saw the soft smile on his face, the loving eyes. I realized this was Chuck's way of telling me not to worry, that he wasn't going to be affected by a miscarriage — he still trusted that God was going to perform a miracle in our lives.

"Oh, Honey, I'm such a fool, such a childish fool! I guess I'll never learn!" I wept in his arms.

"No, dear. You're learning. We are both learning, and I guess the Lord must think we're worth teaching, too, because He's sure trying to get through to us, in spite of us!"

Oh, Father, I marvel at Your patience with us. How often we must learn and re-learn. There seems to be so little carry-over. We see You work, we marvel, but at the next tough spot we make the same mistakes all over again. Our humanity is such a problem. Thank You, Father, for that verse in Psalm 103 which says, "He knoweth our frame He remembereth that we are dust..." Thank You that You know our weaknesses and You love us anyway. You never stop loving us! Praise You, Father!

TRUST

How hard it is for you to learn
to trust the FATHER, Dear;
How much you strain all on your own
to focus all things clear.
You want to see so far ahead—
to travel towards YOUR goal.
You want to be the "Guiding Force, "
"the Captain of your soul."
But GOD would teach you, step by step—
the need to follow HIM.
For life is not all plain and clear—
'tis intricate and dim!
The many pitfalls on its maze
are sure to interfere—
And human understanding needs
much help to persevere.
Mirages to mislead you—
dead-ends to cause delay—
Countless complications —
How could you find the way?
Your FATHER maps the path you tread
from start-point to the end.
HE only asks you follow close

More Complications

> *nor seek to comprehend*
> *The things HE chooses to withhold*
> *until 'tis time to see —*
> *What faith and trust alone reveal —*
> *The will of GOD in thee!*
> *For you will seldom say to GOD,*
> *"I see the way YOU lead."*
> *More often you'll look back and say,*
> *"YOU led, YOU knew my need!"*
> *Just learn the more to trust HIM, Dear.*
> *Depend on HIM for aye!*
> *HE sees ahead — to HIM 'tis clear —*
> *Just follow day by day!*

© *Carol Carlsen–9/4/73*

The phone rang. I rushed to get the key in the front door and ran to catch the phone. Then I froze as I heard the words my sister, Darlene, was saying.

"Daddy has had a massive coronary and is in the cardiac care unit. I'll be right over to pick you up." I raced out the door at the honk of her car horn.

Daddy held my hand and managed a weak smile. "Hi, " he said with difficulty.

"Oh, Daddy, Daddy ..." The doctor explained his condition — the whole anterior portion of his heart was blown; the chances of his pulling through were infinitesimal. If the miracle of survival did occur, the impairment would so restrict him that he, such an active man, would suffer more than living death.

I let my prayer leap to God — "Lord, You have to take him home — he just can't live like this!"

As Mother, Darlene, Chuck and I walked away from the cemetery that day, we were grateful. Daddy might have suffered so much more, but now he was at home in the presence of our Lord. His earthly course was run — unlike us, sorrow couldn't touch him anymore. For a moment, a fleeting thought passed through my mind. Daddy with three babies; one, his own son, Warren, who died in infancy; and my Craig and Christi. I guess that far-away look in my eyes affected Chuck, for he clutched and held me tightly!

Chapter Eighteen
I CLAIM YOUR BLESSING, YOUR PROMISE, GOD

*I*n the days of confusion and adjustment after Daddy's death, I was hardly aware of the slight nausea I was feeling each morning. To further add to my distraction I was kept busy planning and shopping with Darlene, who had become engaged shortly before Daddy's sudden homegoing. This was an exciting time for her, marred only by the knowledge that Daddy would not be there to walk her down the aisle. We enjoyed planning and sharing together. There was a close camaraderie, perhaps the closest of our lives.

Thanksgiving arrived in all its glory! The last thing in the world I could think of was food. I guess that was the first time I started to add up all the sundry symptoms associated with pregnancy and shocked myself.

"Do you think I could be pregnant?" I asked the face in the bathroom mirror, as I stopped brushing my teeth. I grinned a sudsy, toothpaste smile: "You sure feel rotten enough to be!" the face seemed to reply. Throughout that day, baking the pies, roasting the turkeys, eating, conversing with family and guests, cleaning up, the thought kept creeping into my consciousness

"Are you pregnant?" All that week I consciously looked for untoward signs.

I was waiting in the hallway of the lab at Englewood Hospital for my neighbor Susie (the nurse who cared for my dear babies) who had come in for a blood test. The doctor's entrance to the hospital is also located on that corridor. I heard, "What are you doing here?" Henry Saphier's smiling face greeted me.

"Hi! I'm pregnant!" His face dropped to the floor. "You're what!? You're putting me on!"

"Well" I laughed, "I came with Susie for her blood test."

"Whew!" he whistled in relief. "But," I interrupted his peace of mind,

"I'm serious. I really think I might be pregnant!"

"Oh, no!" he said in resignation. "Have you been tested?"

"Not yet."

"Well, let's get it over with." He escorted me into a secretarial office and requested, "My girl thinks she's pregnant. Think you can test her and find out?"

"Oh, Dr. Saphier we'll be delighted to test your daughter."

"D-daughter?" sputtered Henry. "She's not my daughter!" We convulsed into laughter, much to the embarrassment of the poor lab secretary. Henry's only a couple of years older than me and our physical characteristics are just the opposite of each other. There's no way we could be related, but the secretary heard the words "my girl" and assumed it meant "daughter." For several weeks we were the butt of many jokes.

I called Henry's office the following morning.

"Yes, it's true. My God it's true. The test is positive," he said with a tinge of melancholy. "Really?" I could feel the excitement mounting! "I knew it!" "Come in as soon as possible; I'll switch you to the secretary for an appointment. See you."

As I sat on the examining table Henry said, quite solemnly, "Have you considered delivering at a New York City hospital like Columbia, with supportive neo-natal facilities?"

"Do you have privileges at one?" I asked. "I don't want another doctor—so if you're willing, I am too!"

"God help me, God help us both!" Dr. Saphier feigned desperation. "Sure, if you have that much confidence in me. What can I say, except I wish all my patients had your attitude. I really appreciate your courage and trust. Thanks..." his voice trilled off as his eyes traced a pattern on the floor.

"I'm going to put you on a hormone so you won't abort again. Your progesterone level is low; and it's so close to your last pregnancy."

"Will it maintain a defective fetus?" I asked.

"No, if there's a problem in that area, you'll probably abort spontaneously.

"We are going to have a healthy baby this time—I know it." I smiled quietly. Henry patted my back—

"I'll do everything I can!"

Chapter Nineteen
GOD'S PROMISE CONFIRMED

I returned home delirious with joy. "Lord, this is Your miracle," I wrote in my diary of special days, "Today my fifth pregnancy was verified. God, You are the Giver of Life, the Taker also, as I have learned thrice before. I rest in the assurance that my life, as well as our baby's, is in Your hands. You have created us both. My sole confidence rests in 'He doeth all things well.' Grant me total serenity that I may be a witness to all of Your perfect peace, love, and joy in all circumstances of my life. "Thou wilt, keep him in perfect peace whose mind is stayed on Thee — because he trusteth in Thee. Trust ye in the Lord forever for in the Lord Jehovah is everlasting strength' (Isaiah 26:3, 11).

Oh, Lord, I trust in Thee, let me not be ashamed, let not mine enemies triumph over me."

I returned weekly for hormone injections until I realized after several weeks that I appeared to be having a localized reaction to them. When I pointed this out, Dr. Saphier stopped them. No drugs would be needed to sustain this life — only God.

God's Promise Confirmed

As confirmation of His promise, God did something special for me. Chuck and I were at a Couple's Winter Retreat at Tuscarora, the Lutheran Brethren Conference Center in Pennsylvania's Pocono Mountains. Dr. Walter Martin (Founder of Christian Research Institute, and authority on Cults) was the speaker.

I can still remember the living room of the small white cottage, where after the Bible study we quietly adjourned. Dr. Martin explained to me how the healing power of the Lord Jesus could touch us today even as in the days when He walked the earth. He told me of the miracles he had experienced in his own life and ministry, and spoke of the gifts of the Holy Spirit— healing and miracles specifically—that he had seen operate through him and others with first-century power and effect. Dr. Martin asked me if I believed that Christ was able to heal my body and protect my unborn child. He did not ask me if I believed God would—only if He could (Matthew 9:27-30). I told him I did and that I was trusting the Lord for the accomplishment of His will (I John 5:14).

At this point Walter Martin asked Chuck to join with him and together they laid their hands on my head and Dr. Martin prayed, calling on God's love and miraculous power to deliver to us a healthy baby, to heal any defectiveness in my body which might affect its tiny life, and to correct any lung dysfunction (particularly Hyaline Membrane Disease, which could very possibly, as twice before, manifest itself), and to give us perfect confidence that He had heard and had already answered our prayer. Then he spoke prophetically that I would be delivered of a healthy, normal baby and that it would be a boy!

As he spoke the words, my body felt as though a small electric charge had jarred it. The tears started to fall and Chuck gathered me in his arms and embraced me. I could now better understand Luke's account of "But Mary kept all these things and pondered them in her heart." (Luke 2:19 kjv) Thank You, Lord.

My car hardly needed steering; it seemed to know its on way to Dr. Saphier's office, I was there so often for check-ups and tests. Everything was being done to insure a good pregnancy.

At this particular visit Henry gave me an article to read. "Here, he said, "When you're finished we'll talk."

As I read the article I had very odd feelings. It explained that for some reason certain drugs seemed to have positive effects on lung development, among them were addictive narcotics and cortisone.

I laughed when I met Henry. "Do you want to make a dope addict of me? "Hardly. But the steroids...I'd like to put you on Prednizone. His face was serious. "I want to take every practical measure to avoid respiratory problems. My mind was flooded with all that my nursing experience had taught me of cortisone.

"I don't like cortisone. The untoward effects are worse than what its supposed to cure " I stated flatly. "Well, it will be only minimal amounts, and we'll take L-S ratios to see what's happening" (this test is helpful in determining fetal lung development).

I accepted the prescription and started to drive to the pharmacy. I stopped my car in front of it, but I couldn't get out. I could feel my stomach starting to churn. "I don't want to take cortisone' I thought.

For several days that prescription lay in my pocket, and every time I thought of it, my stomach churned again. My sister called from California and I shared my feelings with her and her husband. He prayed quietly (long distance) that as each of us sought the Lord for His will, we would each receive an answer and that the answers would all agree.

I was socked between the eyes. I had never prayed about this; I just made up my mind that I didn't want to take the Predizone and that was that.

"Lord, I know You care about every minute detail, even to the numbering of the hairs of my head. This isn't minute, Lord. It could seriously damage me or the baby, or both of us, and I'm sorry I've stewed so long because I've been so stupid in not coming to You with this. Let me know in no uncertain terms what to do!"

God didn't write me a letter or do any other spectacular thing for an answer—He just let me have insomnia that night. Funny thing, but all I could think about was why I liked Henry Saphier as a doctor, and why, in spite of what happened, I continued to go to him.

"Please, Father, let me sleep. I'm so tired... (yawn) Henry Saphier—I have confidence in him, I trust him—I don't want another doctor.

"Father, You know I've put this whole pregnancy in Your hands and Henry, too; I've committed him to You to guide and direct..." Then it clicked.

"Oh, yes Father, I see what You're driving at—I can trust Henry's judgment because I've entrusted him to You, Okay, I'll fill that prescription...

I can't remember another thing because I peacefully slept the rest of that night.

The phone rang the next morning. Darlene's voice was as close as next door,

"Hi, how are you?" "You're going to take that medicine, right?"

"How did you know?" I asked in astonishment.

"We prayed, and got a 'yes'—are we agreed?" There's a unique joy that fills one solely at those times when God answers prayer and it's happened practically immediately—no waiting involved. Wow!

As my due date approached, Henry started to get more and more solicitous. I felt like I, was going to that office almost continuously. My due date passed, and he became a bit impatient.

"I'm scheduling you for July 12th."

"But I want to start labor naturally, before you operate."

"I know. But it's so risky, and you're already overdue."

What could I do but resign myself to surgery? "Father, I entrusted him to You. I want to go into labor because then I'll know for sure it's Your time for the baby, but You work it out...

Again, there were no neon signs or divine utterances about God's will—just a miserable case of bronchitis and severe upper respiratory congestion. Dr. Saphier tried several medications, to no avail. I continued to cough and blow and wheeze.

"Carol, we can't operate with all that congestion—we'll reschedule, but I'd like to do a paracentesis" (the removal of fluid from the placenta, which when tested reveals many vital things about the new life it bathes). "Be prepared to stay: it may initiate labor," the doctor said, when I arrived for the test several days later. This time I wasn't ready, for after twelve hours I went home.

"Your timing, Lord, Your timing...

Chapter Twenty

THE CHILD OF PROMISE

Saturday, July 27th, dawned, and as I awoke, the first conscious thought through my brain proclaimed, "This is the day the Lord hath made—rejoice and be glad in it!"

The bronchitis was over and Henry had rescheduled the Caesarian section. The results of the testing of the amniotic fluid from the parascentesis had indicated the baby's lungs were mature and all appeared well. I was to go into the hospital and be given a drug, which was able to initiate labor, then be put on a monitor to measure contractions so at the precise time I could be brought into surgery with the least risk to me or my baby.

The air of excitement in my house was stupendous. I got dressed and rechecked my suitcase. As I sat down to drink my cup of black coffee (food was forbidden as surgery was imminent), the 21st Psalm besieged my brain:

> *"Shall I lift up mine eyes unto the hills*
> *for my help? No!*
> *My help cometh from the Lord*
> *Which made heaven and earth.*
> *He will not suffer thy foot to be moved.*
> *He that keepeth thee will not slumber,*

> *He that keepeth (Henry) Israel shall neither*
> *Slumber nor sleep. The Lord is thy keeper..." (kjv)*

Funny, but that "Henry" just seemed to sneak in there... Dr. Saphier's full name is Henry Israel Saphier. And, as untheological as it may seem, it further confirmed to me that God was in total control. It was just that added bit of assurance that took any slight apprehension away before it could blossom into worry and fear.

The verse just played itself over and over again, with the same "Henry" error, much like a tune you can't stop humming—it was just grooved into my subconscious. I shared my new rendition with Henry as I climbed onto the hospital bed.

"Well, the Lord is our only help...and your faith helps me," he said slowly, and his eyes looked down. I can't help wondering what else he was thinking at that moment.

Then the tension in my hospital room was great, as Dr. Saphier rushed in and out, checking the monitors for the precise moment for surgery. The tension also showed in Chuck's face as he pondered what the outcome would be.

"I love you, Honey—always remember how much I love you!" His eyes clouded over. "Now—" snapped Henry, "we're there, let's go!" Chuck bent down and gathered me as close as he could. He kissed me as he had never done before—it was almost as if he was afraid it would be the last time and he was unwilling to let me go.

"Come on, Chuck," called Susie, my private nurse, "Let's wait out here."

"You can stand just outside the operating room door, Chuck," Henry called, as he wheeled me past.

The operating room had five doctors scrubbed and waiting; two obstetricians, the Chief of Anesthesiology, another anesthesiologist, and Dr. Bell, my pediatrician, plus a couple of nurses. "Wow! I said, slightly amazed, "You are really first class!"

"Yeah," said Henry, "You wouldn't get better service if you were a queen!"

Small talk was made concerning how many nationalities were represented. Then they were ready. As the anesthesia mask was fitted over my face, the last thing I heard, whether spoken by someone in that operating room or by the Father Himself, was a resounding "BE STILL AND KNOW THAT I AM GOD!"

When I awoke not too many moments later, as I was given a minimal amount of anesthesia (the baby didn't appear to have gotten any because Henry worked so quickly).

Henry said, "What are you going to call your son?"

I was thrilled. "A son? Oh God, a son, I can't believe it! Thank You, thank You!"

At that very moment Dr. Bell was personally delivering our new "Charles Richard Carlsen, Jr." to New York's Columbia Presbyterian Babies Hospital and Chuck was with him. Also, these two doctors had covered every angle possible, even to the calling of the New York/New Jersey Port Authority and having a lane of the George Washington Bridge closed off to be available for swift crossing of the ambulance from New Jersey to New York!

Later that day Dr. Bell stopped by my room. "I've just spoken with Columbia. So far no sign of any problems!"

"And this time there are not going to be any!" I smiled. I can't remember anything other than falling confidently asleep that night. The next morning I could scarcely believe what had happened. It was rather like a dream—here I was in the very same room I'd been in last year, the same nurses were coming in and out, congratulating me, telling me they were praying, too.

Henry came in smiling. "Hey, we did alright! Everything still looks good!"

"That's great," but my voice was less than enthusiastic. "Hey, what's the matter? Want to check for yourself?" and he dialed the neonatologist's number at Columbia.

"Yes, Mrs. Carlsen. He's just fine. Such a beautiful boy, the biggest of our census. We're still testing, however..." I closed my eyes and smiled; but the tears flowed and I didn't know why.

Later that day an excited voice spoke over the telephone. "And you know what? I got to see li'l Chuck before you did! Ha, ha!" My nine-year-old, Cheryl, teased. She, Chuck, and all the grandparents had gone to Columbia to see our baby.

"He's a nice baby and you should see—he has his own nurse, just for him, and a rocking chair, and the nurse has a swing to swing him in if he cries..." she went on and on so dramatically that she nearly burst. Now I knew what was wrong. As I hung up the phone I realized that my deep feelings were subconsciously denying that I had had a boy, simply because I hadn't seen him!

Now I knew it had to be true; I remembered, "a little child shall lead them." Susie was just ecstatic.

"Can you believe it? Dr. Bell wants me to go and pick up li'l Chuck and bring him here to Englewood. They're discharging him from Columbia! Can you believe it? Oh, Carol, it's so wonderful!" I sat quietly in my room looking at the many beautiful flowers that had arrived. There was a soft tap on my door.

"Carol, he's coming up now," the nurse said excitedly.

I tried to get out of bed as quickly as my surgery would permit me, but it was not fast enough. I heard such a commotion you would hardly believe it was a hospital. As I got to the door there was an entourage walking toward me. I think every nurse on the staff was there, surrounding our Susie who was embracing a wee blue bundle.

"Here he is," Susie said, just as proud as can be. "Isn't he beautiful?" "My baby! My baby!"

The Child Of Promise

The nurses said they could put a lampshade on me, I was glowing so.

"Can I hold him?" I asked. "Well, Mrs. Keady (head Pediatric Nurse) said to bring him straight to the Nursery, but we won't tell her," Susie quipped, her blue eyes twinkling. She placed that precious blue bundle in my arms.

"He's really here, he's really mine," and the tears started to fall again. I watched as Susie carried my li'l Chuck down the corridor until the doors separating the nursery closed behind them. The tears still flowed, for the magnitude of my joy could not be contained. As I sat quietly alone, I reflected back to God's promise, the promise I had dared to believe—"Children are My blessing...I will build your house..."

"Oh, Father, You outdid Yourself! You answered far beyond what I could have ever imagined! And a boy! Why, that's just like a frosting on the cake..."

A boy, my thoughts were suddenly drawn up short—the prophecy of Dr. Martin emblazoned itself across my consciousness. My body reacted with a peculiar shiver and I sat there stunned. I had believed God for a baby, I had believed Him for a healthy baby, but I guess in the back of my mind I felt that believing Him for a healthy boy baby would just be expecting too much.

"Oh, Father, my faith, even though it was too small, didn't limit You." Here again I realized God's love, His giving, His goodness has nothing to do with me or what I do for Him. It has only to do with Him, for He doesn't just have love, HE IS LOVE. Li'l Chuck was indeed the child of promise, a prophesied promise! The realization of what had transpired brought me a far deeper awareness of just how detailed God's plan for my life was.

The next evening was the initiation of a new hospital policy, "Father's Hour," and at nine o'clock the nurses brought li'l Chuck to his Daddy and me. As we held him we prayed a prayer of praise and thanksgiving to the Lord, who had given him to us and had taught us both a new way of life—victorious life! "I have come that they might have life—and that more abundantly..." "There is sorrow for a season, but Joy cometh in the morning." (Psalm 30:5 kjv)

And Linda, I wouldn't trade what God has taught me for anything I had before! Also, have you considered the worth of the investment you've just forwarded to glory? Part of you, YOU, is already in Jesus' presence!! You'll have someone to welcome you when you arrive. (My welcoming committee is a wee bit larger.) Think about it!

It is easy to look back and see where we have been. It takes faith to go ahead to the unknown and faith is RESPONSIBILITY — my RESPONSE to God's ABILITY! I can walk confidently, holding His hand, or use my hands to cover my eyes and grope by myself. Either way, He is THERE. I make the difference by what I do with my hands!

Bless you! May you discover too, that "God's love surrounds you like a cloud, and nothing can get to you unless it goes through Him first!"

Love,
Carol

POSTLOGUE

I had just finished the letter and signed my name when I felt I should share some scripture with Linda. As I thumbed through those well-worn pages I was not quite prepared for what I found. You see, God had still another fantastic discovery for me. My eyes fell on some scribbling in the margin next to Philippians 3:10. There I had written "MY GOAL OF 1971, 1/1/71," and I had underlined half of that tenth verse—"That I may know HIM and the POWER of His resurrection..." (kjv)

My thoughts went back to that New Year's Day. I remember how depressed I was and how seemingly meaningless life had become. Something was very wrong. There was no joy in my Christian life, nor could I see much in the lives of many others of my acquaintance. I was so busy working and doing, but what I was accomplishing brought short-lived satisfaction. That particular day I recall vividly a sentence of scripture from I Corinthians 15: "We are of all men most miserable." It kept plaguing me. However out of context it was, it surely described my Christian experience. For many weeks I had been thinking, "If this is all there is to Christianity, is it worth it?" Oh, I had had other times similar to this, but I either talked myself out of them or suppressed them beneath a plastic smile, accepted theological vocabulary and a seemingly "happy" Christian exterior. This time, it wouldn't be suppressed, nor could I talk myself out of it.

The most logical course of action was to face it head on and decide what to do about it. I know enough of the Bible, and enough about the personality of God, not to accuse God of making me miserable. Therefore, the only conclusion had to be that I was somehow the cause. "There has to be more to this Christian life that I have, God—show me, help me!"

My prayer was more academic than emotional. I would try hard to find out more about why I didn't have the kind of life I thought I should have. I would start reading my Bible more often and have sort of regular "quiet times."

Hence, coming upon Philippians 3:10, I made my New Year's Resolution...

Now I was re-reading it in the Amplified Bible. It said something incredible to me; it said, "(For my determined purpose is) that I may know Him—that I may progressively become more deeply and intimately acquainted with Him, perceiving and recognizing and understanding (the wonders of His Person) more strongly and more clearly. And that I may in that same way come to know the POWER outflowing from His resurrection (which it exerts over believers)." I stopped there as the tears started to fall.

"You answered that prayer, Lord, You really, truly answered it!" "Read on, read on," something inside compelled. Obediently I read on, sometimes unable to see as I blinked back the tears. ... and that I may so share His sufferings as to be continually transformed (in Spirit into His likeness even) to His death, (in the hope) that if possible I may attain to the (spiritual and moral) resurrection (that lifts me) out from among the dead (even while in the body). Not that I have now attained (this ideal) or am already made perfect, but I press on to lay hold of and make my own that for which. Christ Jesus, the Messiah, has laid hold of me and made me His own" (Philippians 3:10-12). I had stopped underlining just before the "suffering" part. Something seemed to say now, "Carol, knowing Me intimately costs something; knowing my power requires something! You can't have My glory without My suffering; you can't truly live until you deny yourself—die to yourself, and live unto Me!" I had read that portion of scripture before and just slid over it because it hadn't made any sense. Now I was understanding that I had to come to know Him in a vital, deep way, that I had come to experience that Power of His resurrection...His Holy Spirit within me, that I had entered into His sufferings—that I had shared in His death because it should have been my death— and to all intents and purposes the "old Adam," "Carol," had died and the new "creature in Christ," "Carol," had been made alive. His POWER—the Holy Spirit—had quickened me to live a productive, ongoing, ever-growing Christian life, manifesting the fruits and gifts of His Spirit so necessary for such a life. And that it was a continuous process—that I could be, and in all actuality was, truly becoming the person God wanted me to be; and finally, that although I wasn't perfect in the past nor am I perfect now, I can forget those imperfect things as something forgiven and covered over by Jesus' blood, and therefore "press on toward the goal, for the prize of the high calling of God, in Jesus Christ." (Philippians 8:14 kjv)

THE FRUITS OF THE SPIRIT

"Take my life and let it be
Consecrated, Lord, to Thee."
These words I sang from deep within,
My soul's desire, to live for Him;
Eagerly I asked for LOVE
Overflowing from courts above.
Next for JOY petitioned I
With PEACE and PATIENCE satisfy
A GENTLE SPIRIT, BENEVOLENT HEART

And FAITHFULNESS to me impart;
HUMILITY and SELF-CONTROL—
Perfect in me a Christlike soul...
I didn't know for what I prayed
But Father heard full well;
He meant to answer in His way
But how, He would not tell.
For had I known the true degree
Of my petition then,
The tutelage He planned for me
Would overwhelm, transcend.
He answered not with perfect gifts
As I had planned He would;
He answered not with instant fruits
Although I thought He should.
I asked for LOVE, He gave instead
A grievous situation;
I found my bitter self immersed.
In woeful tribulation.
The love I sought could only come
When I found His compassion;
And in the night of storm and grief
My soul knew His refashion.
God is love and He alone
Could take this selfish heart,
Implant His nature in my own,
Benevolence impart.

The JOY I sought was not the one
That Father planned for me;
The transient pleasures of the day
When all went -perfectly,
The happiness of all I want,
Fulfillment of desire,
Would disappear without a trace

In life's oft-scorching fire.
Instead He taught that perfect joy
Which changeless stands the test
In every wave of circumstance
  Triumphant and at rest.

And what of PEACE? That tranquil state
That calm through tempest gales
Could it be mine apart from Him
Whose voice each fear assails?
Peace, Be still, to wind and wave
  He speaks within my soul;
My being knows serenity
  Immersed in His control.
"Thou wilt give him perfect peace,
  Whose mind is stayed on Thee;"
Words of comfort, sure and true,
  To trust eternally.

Then PATIENCE, ah, illusive thing,
  For which I strove in vain.
Apart from tribulation
  Forbearance cannot train.
The schoolroom for this gracious fruit—
  I shun to enter there;
But He who teaches all things well
  Compels me sojourn there
And learn to trust His love for me
  Despite sore circumstance;
Nor ask that He remove it
  Until the time He plans.

A GENTLE SPIRIT, BENEVOLENT HEART,
  What fiber makes me such?
The one that woven in with tears

Will soothe abrasion's touch;
The Master weaves my tenuous threads
To fashion His design.
He cuts and pulls the filaments
To make each one align.
Conforming to His Image,
Reflecting God above,
And spreading over those I meet
His great, transcendent love.

FAITHFULNESS, ah, faithfulness,
Sweet treasure, highest goal;
The means by which our lives
Assess fidelity of soul.
Single-minded constancy
In all I say and do,
Trustworthiness and loyalty,
A servant tried, yet true.
He gives the gift—still I must choose
Amidst the daily din.
To exercise oft stubborn will
And yield my all to Him.
The striving for HUMILITY
Cannot be sought as prize,
For 'tis the golden offspring
Of a life of sacrifice.
Giving thought to others,
Quenching haughty pride,
Making meekness paramount,
And arrogance subside,
Esteeming one another
For love and not reward,
Gently building unity
In the body of our Lord.

SELF-CONTROL takes total charge
In waves of strong emotion.
It wills one temperate, calm, and
Still, amidst the grand commotion;
Restrains desires oft passion-filled,
Allows no "ruffled feathers,"
Contains indulgence tightly bound,
Impetuousness it tethers.
Can I by strength of my own will
Command myself be so?
When self-control means HIS control
He'll cause this fruit to grow!
© Carol A. Carlsen 1977

ABOUT THE AUTHOR

Mrs. Carlsen lives in California with her husband, Chuck, of 52 years. Her two children and their spouses live in close proximity. She has two grandchildren and a great grandchild due to arrive in February.

Mrs. Carlsen is a graduate of Wagner College in Staten Island, NY where she attended both the School of Nursing and the School of Education. She held Teaching Credentials in New York and New Jersey. When she moved to California, she held California Teaching and Administration Credentials. She retired in 2009 after 48 years as an Educator.

www.ingramcontent.com/pod-product-compliance
Ingram Content Group UK Ltd.
Pitfield, Milton Keynes, MK11 3LW, UK
UKHW022216230426
12048UKWH00016BA/883